MW01487983

Her Hope

by, Lynnette Marie Lopez

This publication contains the opinions and ideas of its author. It is intended to provide helpful and informative material on the subjects addressed in the publication. The author and publisher specifically disclaim all responsibility for any liability, loss, or risk, personal or otherwise, which is incurred as a consequence, directly or indirectly, of the use and application of any of the contents of this book.

WRITERS REPUBLIC L.L.C.
515 Summit Ave. Unit R1
Union City, NJ 07087, USA

Website: *www.writersrepublic.com*
Hotline: *1-877-656-6838*
Email: *info@writersrepublic.com*

Ordering Information:
Quantity sales. Special discounts are available on quantity purchases by corporations, associations, and others. For details, contact the publisher at the address above.

Library of Congress Control Number:		2020949792
ISBN-13:	978-1-64620-770-1	[Paperback Edition]
	978-1-64620-771-8	[Digital Edition]

Rev. date: 11/02/2020

Contents

Thank you grandma, for being my constant hope.
And thank you dad, for being my reason to keep hanging on to hope.

for the ones with hope,
unspoken words, radical
thoughts, obsessions, scars,
smiles, laughs, and hope.

her love that
never ended

fall

I'm falling for you
Faster than the leaves turn orange and red
Harder than the way the leaves touch the ground
I'm falling for you
And i can't seem to get you out of my head
you are the leaves in my mind spinning around
And around,
And around ...
And around.
But I'm still falling for you
Don't let it spook you, but I'm just so into you
It's fall season.
But don't be afraid to fall too,
I'm picking up your leaf at the end of the night

naked for you

hey , do you dare me ?

i'm about to show you all of me

can you handle it ?

don't be scared

tell me you want all of me please

you

I pick you , i choose you
I want you . i'm holding you
I love you

let me show you that it's you
please , come in

I love you
let me love you all the way through

it's you
i'll show you that it's you

weak

you make me weak

you make me feel soft and bubbly

and filled with butterflies

with you , it's literally like im floating on air

I have no idea how to describe the way you make me feel .

you have so much power and control over me

i just melt when you look into my eyes

you have this hold over me that makes me just fall

fall straight into love with you

fall hard

i just want to fall into your arms

hold me , baby me , cuddle me , kiss me .. please

you make me weak

you make me feel soft and bubbly

and filled with butterflies

you make me weak

carnival ride

maybe i just have too much fun
no fear, and filled with the urge to do
the fastest wildest things
taking risks and doing the most out of everyone

"let's go on a carnival ride," i said.
and so we did.

I grabbed her hand and felt it tighten. I
told her "don't be scared, i got you."

i held her through every twist and turn, i looked her in the
eyes after and told her we would do this with our eyes closed
and our hands in the air next time. "You're crazy," she said.

"It's a roller coaster everyday with you," she said.

roller coaster

maybe i have a fear of letting go
fearing the worst, being pessimistic
but it's okay to go slow
just don't go to fast it might make you sick

"I hate rollercoasters," i said
but then we went.

I grabbed her hand out of fear and squeezed it with
all my might. she told me that she's got me.

she held me through every bit of it. at the end, she looked
me in the eyes and said "next time we do this with our eyes
closed and our hands in the air" i told her she was crazy.

"It's just a carnival ride babe," she said.

honest

just be honest
have good intentions
just be in the right
have good in your heart and mind
don't break me
don't hurt me
just be honest
tell me what you want
show me how you want it
just be honest
have good intentions
please

vending machines

stepping up to the vending machines
ones broken.
no ones noticed yet,
but you did.
you took once, it was free.
came back,
still broken and unnoticed,
but you knew.
you took again,
why not? it was good.
you enjoyed it.
taking without giving, not paying.
thats what you did to my heart.

you stepped up to me
saw my breaks, read my hurt.
you took my care,
took my time, my attention & love
saw i was still broken,
but yet, you took again.
stole pieces of my heart
you enjoyed it.
taking without giving, not caring.
thats what you did.

lovers nervosa

purging

binging

chills down my spine

face pale, cheeks burning

holding my stomach

squeezing my thighs

hair tied

hands holding on

purging

binging

on your love

her mind and heart and body

the today

the flashbacks are aggressive today

they're pushing on my stomach and scratching at my sides

it's making me starve after I've purged it all down

the flashbacks are aggressive today

the dysmorphia is raging today

it looks like my arms are bone-thin today
and my thighs are sticks

my stomach is getting bigger and my
chin is forming another one

the dysmorphia is raging today

the depression got worse today

they're forcing me to isolate myself and push people away

it's made me cry and scream into the void for help

the depression worsened today

the anxiety hit badly today

it shaking my hands so hard they're aching in pain

they're making my throat close, my tears
stream fast and body faint

the anxiety hit badly today

wrong wrong wrong

why are you following me?

let go of my arm

You tickling me isn't funny

im laughing cause im scared

leave me alone please

don't touch me

get away

im trying to walk away , can't you tell ?

the closer you're getting is scaring me

how do i make you go away

we were just fine a few minutes ago

why do you want this?

I don't want this

please don't touch me

im uncomfortable

let me go

stop touching my hand

don't rip my jeans

stop

no

this is wrong

wrong wrong wrong

fine fine fine

she's walking away from me , why ?

im just trying to hold her

she's laughing ? that means she likes it

she's saying no but i don't care

why would i leave you alone?

don't push me away

or walk away from me

let me get closer , you'll be fine

im not going away

You've been fine all this time ?

why you acting so weird all of a sudden

you want this

you really do , don't deny it

let me without saying please

I don't want to let go

im gonna grab your hand now

I don't care

im gonna rip your jeans

yeah

yes

this is fine

fine fine fine

once again

I remind myself to not walk alone at night
don't let a creepy man follow you in the grocery store
I remind myself to not make eye contact
don't follow anyone you don't know
I remind myself to not go into someone's car
don't listen to the scary man nearby

but once again
it's someone i know
a friend
took advantage of the fact that I was smiling and laughing
thought he was good enough
took my hand and held it when i tried to pull away
grabbed me when i tried to push him off
picked me up when I squirmed to get out of his grip
once again
it's someone i thought i knew
not a friend
once again

full on panic

i'm freaking out
full on panic
an attack on my mind is happening
nothing might go right
everything might go wrong
i'm freaking out
how bad can things go ?
who knows, honestly
will my friends judge me ?
do i even understand what i'm doing
cause this might all go bad
i'm freaking out
full on panic

attack in panic

she heard it coming from miles away
pounding and pounding , drowning out all other sound .
until the lights got brighter and the sirens started ringing .
panic
panic
panic
it was on its way
attack
attack
attack
the ground started trembling uncontrollably
rain started pouring from the skies while thunder roared
lightning was striking and damaging the walls and trees
panic
panic
panic
its here
attack
attack
attack
everything imploded in on her
the walls caved in and the smoke filled the air
everything went silent
panic attack

panic attack

panic attack

sudden breeze

the air was hot
burning on your skin
tense and warm
filled with anger
one hundred degrees of madness
then a sudden breeze flew in
and brought that smile
your hair flew all directions
filled with happiness
a flower passed by your ear
singing with joy
then the heat was back
it came in just as sudden as the breeze did
humid and rigid
it touched your skin roughly
and wet with hate
the sudden breeze came right before the rain
to remind you of the calm
before the storm.
the storm blew in
raining and lightning
with the thunder shouting loudly in your ears
the drips from the clouds crying
filled with sadness

the rain left, but the flood didn't.
the post storm rainbow gave you a slight smile
reminding you that a sudden breeze was coming.
this time the breeze stayed.

her love she

gave

newfound

you are my newfound

newfound

/ˈn(y)o͞ofound/

adjective

recently discovered or established.

my newfound future ,

my newfound song ,

my newfound heart ,

run , laugh , dance ,

my newfound life ,

safety , sound , and

my newfound love

a million years ago our stars didn't align , they hit and
crossed each other for what felt like centuries . the
meteor finally moved . the sun shone through and our
stars aligned . we aligned . it was a new discovery . a new
sight . something bright . something strong in the sunrising
sky . the sky was just rising . but our stars were still
shining bright turning the early morning mist into
rainbows . the skies promising to keep us together .

the newfound stars laughed and smiled all day and
night . their light never burning out , never fading

, never . cause these stars won't . blessed newfound stars . they walked into love together .

don't.

don't make it look like you're victim. there is no victim here.

there's only us learning more and more about each
other as we go. we'll both make mistakes, but this is
all part of it , you of all people should know this.

don't question me. if you're curious or
want reassurance , just tell me

don't interrogate me.

don't doubt my love for you.

don't second think my commitment.

don't question if my love is real.

this is trust.

i have all my trust in you, and im trusting that you do the same.

if you want me to do something, if you want to hear something.

tell. me.

ask. me.

we will get nowhere if you don't communicate.

this is me communicating. this is me
expressing. this is me communicating.

why raise your suspicions?

why question?

but why did i defend myself? because i stand my ground.

I will never stop fighting. for. me.
i will defend my actions and i will defend
who i am and how i do things.

because who is to anyone why?

maybe to you, why? right?

you want to know why?

okay, i'll tell you why.

because just like you have reasons from your past as
to why you do or don't do certain things, i'm the same
way. I have my reasons as to why i "defend" myself.

because i do the best i can to show the way i feel

 to show that us is just you and me.

to show that i care about you.

to show that i am faithful to you, loyal
to you, and trusting in you.

and most of all to show that i love you. and only you.

what else can i do? how else am i supposed to do this?

how do i love you right?

in the way that you want me to?

please do tell, because right now i think
im just getting it al wrong.

purple pink

colors and colors and colors
so many to choose from
colors and colors and colors
yet you find a way to choose a least
favorite and a great favorite

colors and colors and colors
purple being me
green being you
colors and colors and colors

colors and colors and colors
i see pink on you
you see red on me
colors and colors and colors

the universe has colors that aren't even on the scale yet
colors and colors and colors
how deep can the color purple go?
colors and colors and colors
how much baby colors are there?

colors and colors and colors
never anything in just black and white
colors and colors and colors

Lynnette Marie Lopez

ones with different shades and hues

colors and colors and colors
you are the color in my life
filling my everyday with a new color
colors and colors and colors

purple pink faded with army olive green type writer font
chosen from colors and colors and colors

colors and colors and colors

race

you beat me . you ran into love , while i was walking into it .

the race is long and i wanted to pace myself and
take my time , but you wanted to run .

we're a team . and teams have to run together . i was holding
you back , but you were too strong and kept going anyway .

i had no more energy to run , but you had it all .

It would have been unfair if i stayed in
the race and made you lose .

i didn't match the love you gave . and that's unfair to you .

you deserve someone that is going to
be cheering you on in the race

someone that is going to love you just as
much or even more than you do them .

you deserve more than me .

more than someone that gives up mid race .

i didn't want to give up , but you said we're done .

we lost .

and i left the race .

you beat me . you ran into love , while i was walking into it .

pink

you remind me of pink
a soft, light, baby pink
sunrise on a fresh morning,
pink rays of light shining on your red hair

you hate the color pink
so, you'd rather be green
a hard, rough, sturdy green
leaves that fall from the trees in your favorite season

but you still remind me of pink
soft, light, and baby
sitting in a thick warm blanket,
waiting for her juice box to be opened

yet you still hate the color pink
hard, rough, and sturdy
saying you're in control
pinning old leaves up against a wall, oh and your girlfriend too

you remind me of pink
a soft, light, baby pink
But you'd rather be green
a hard, rough, sturdy green

maybe

maybe i should fight for your love back

maybe i should give up and let you be .

maybe i should try and confess everything

maybe im being a fuck girl .

maybe im being an attention whore again
and im being a terrible person

but one thing for sure i know i cant do
, is get you out of my head .

i want you here .

but i dont know how to express that properly

i just dont want to lose a chance

i dont want to miss a shot

tell me i have no chance

tell me not to shoot

you say , but -

you say you love me ,

but do you want my love ?

you say falling in love with you is a mystery ,

well are you gonna let me solve it ?

you say you won't make it easy for me ,

but was it ever ?

you say i can shoot my shot ,

but who's to say i'll miss ?

you say i have a second chance ,

but what if i ruin it ?

you say you love me ,

but do you want my love ?

don't deserve

what is it that you say you want ?

you want me ? you want an us ?

no.

you of all people do not deserve that anymore

no.

what do you expect from me ?

my love ? my attention ?

no.

you do not get to sit there and take
advantage of all that i have to give

no.

but lucky for me , i don't care one bit about what you want

yes.

because what you want you don't deserve anymore

no.

you don't deserve me.

his endless words

soft heart

you're making my heart soft
stahp
i'm boutta catch some feelings
i'm bout to fall in love or something
you're making my heart soft

you have a soft smile
it curves one way more than the other
you never show your teeth when you smile
and your hair poofs up in the mornings
you have a lot of respect,
but you also like to take risks and rebel sometimes
you laugh softly and not loud and long like i do
you have a soft smile

you're making my heart soft
stahp
cause i'm really catching feelings now
i'm really falling in love now
you got my heart soft

8 letters

i love you

living for every moment with you

overflowing with smiles and giggles

vibrant but subtle with your voice

enchantingly charming in the way you look at me

you are the only one i want

obsessing over your smile , gosh i cant get over it

up and down and all around , the butterflies are wild

8 letters

fire, storm, art

you have a fire in your heart
when you smile it burns brighter
and when you laugh it burns harder
the fire itself is better than any art

you have a storm in your mind
when you cry, it rains in tears
and when you're sad it thunders
oh, this storm .. i promise you don't need to hide behind

let the fire burn
let the fire explode
let me see you smile
let me hear that laugh
your fire is art

let the storm pour
let the storm ruin
let me show you, that you're okay
let me show you, that i'm here
your storm is art

you have a fire in your heart
you have a storm in your mind

Lynnette Marie Lopez

your fire is art
your storm is art

fire, storm, art
laugh, cry, art

sunrise and sunset

i wake up early to see the sunrise sometimes,
all i can think about is seeing it with you.
you sleep late and don't see the sunset,
you aren't awake for the sunrise either,
but i wish you'd take a glimpse at one at least.

rapping things for him

listen

baby, i gotta tell you something,

and i gotta tell it fast before i let it spill

remember the days we used to sit back and just chill?

back when we had all the money and the time to kill

giving me kisses, got the butterflies in
my stomach just not holding still

and at every other word, you say you got me blushing

got my heart pumping

got the blood rushing

got the simple thought of you just running round my head

got me spinning and thinkin, now my cheeks are turning red

reminiscing on the nights i got you tangled up in bed

drinking pink martinis, looking from the heights

thinking you'd be forever, yes baby you just might

let's travel the world, and let this love take flight

I swear it won't be a fright

baby, you're such a beautiful sight

i promise you will be alright by my side

as long as the knot is tied, baby, you'll be mine

but baby, now that it's late, let's kick
back and let me dive in your divine

tell me, love, is this a sign?

will a new chapter come in our storyline?

and please tell me if i'm starting to sound dumb

because

um

um

um

i'm running out of things to say

but baby please don't go astray

i was just trying to make you my bae

so come on baby, let's go this way

follow the roses, i know it's a cliche

baby, you don't even have to meet me halfway

where are you

where are you ..
on this orange night .
driving down a long empty road ?
or in bed holding your pillow ?

where are you ..
when the sun is setting .
taking one last picture before dark sets in ?
or peeking through the blinds waiting for dark ?

on this orange night
when the sun is setting
where are you

lessons i wish i didn't have to learn

you were a stranger

with a spark in his eyes

and a fire in his heart

shy with an outgoing personality

destructive dark past

but seeking a bright golden future

with fame and music

a wife and kids

those words i helped you rhyme

and the tears i caught from your eyes

the time i had

and the chances i gave

meant nothing to you

when you slammed my heart on my driveway

sweeping up my broken pieces

learning a lesson i wish i didn't have to

wondering if you could change

that night i admitted i still loved you

watching you walk away

leaving nothing you wanted

i was ignoring the truth hoping it was just a bad dream

but it was a lesson i wish i didn't have to learn

showed my scars while trying to heal yours

read you my damage and attempted to fix yours

changed for you, expecting for you to do the same

i was wrong and you were perfect

in ways i wish you weren't

you were-

you are, perfectly imperfect

someone that i saw all the good in,

when all you showed me was the bad.

her rainbow over her head

not boys

can't say how I truly feel
I'm unsure of what they'll all think or say, or do.
no matter what, this feeling is still there.
forever here.
I push you away so you don't find out.
but why hide it?

they're all so gorgeous
no no no, not boys. girls.
girls with long flowy hair, painted nails,
button-up shirts, converse and vans.

I shouldn't feel this way, but I do.
how can I ignore this feeling? I can't resist
I'm supposed to like boys with muscles and short cut hair,
but she walks by with a look in her eye that says "follow me"
how can I not enjoy this? how am I
supposed to pretend to like boys?
when I like girls.
this isn't a phase
this isn't for attention.
It's girls.

they're all so gorgeous
no no no, not boys. girls.

girls with long flowy hair, painted nails,
button-up shirts, converse and vans.

let me love who I want?

what does it matter who I love, or who I kiss

I don't choose this

this isn't a mistake

I'm gonna love

who I want

they're all so gorgeous

no no no, not boys. girls.

girls with long flowy hair, painted nails,
button-up shirts, converse and vans.

they're all so gorgeous

no no no, not boys. girls.

girls with long flowy hair, painted nails,
button-up shirts, converse and vans.

accept

can you ?

maybe ?

one day ?

 for a second ?

maybe just a moment ?

a small moment

you can forget all about it afterwards

it'll be quick , i "promise"

i won't even say the word ..

i won't

i won't

i won't

but does it hurt ?

cause it hurts me

do you care?

cause i wish i could stop

does it disturb you?

cause your ugly looks are getting disturbing

does it bother you?

cause the way you're acting is bothering me

please?

may you?

one day?

for a second?

just a moment?

a small one

accept me.

for every part of me.

even the ones you dislike and hate so much.

accept me.

for me. and all of me please.

please.

please.

please.

real and true

i have to be real and true to who i am

i've been in fear of who i am

fear that no one will accept me

but i accept me now

and my own personal acceptance is all i need

i'm going to be real and true to who i am

i don't need validation from anyone anymore

not from my friends, not from society

not from my dad, and not from my mom

bwcause i accept me.

lesbian me.

gay me.

queer me.

pansexual me.

bisexual me.

no label me.

every label me.

just me.

me.

i accept me.

and that's all i need.

to be real and true to me.

finally me

i'm finally me
cutting my hair
changing my name
discovering my style
finding my label
i'm finally me

i'm finally me
girly boy short hair
i go by lynnee
soft e girl with spice aesthetic
pansexual
i'm finally me

her with the blue eyes

love Cliff

there's this cliff i stood on when i met you . i
wanted to end my life . but you set a trap of love
at the bottom of the cliff . you saved me .
my sister had a rope tied around my waist so i
wouldn't fall to my death . she pulls and pulls
everyday to make sure i don't fall to my death .
but once i told her i met you . she let go . she saw
the trap you placed . she saw bottomless death
at the end of the cliff turn into love . she told me
i have another reason to stay .
you saved me . you came into my life and
pushed me so fast off that cliff and i fell into love
with you . so fast because you put so much love
in me , it weighed me down in a good way and
i've fallen in love . with you . and now you say
you've fallen too . but you're leaving . how can
you leave ? why ? did i have to fall for you ? why

did you push me ? why did you make me fall in
love with you ? i'm crying . but i've fallen . i've
reached the bottom . but there's more . i still
have more to go . i still have more time with you ,
i will still fall more and more into love with you
every second .

you gave me one more reason to stay . and now i
don't want to leave . i don't want you to leave .
you gave me a new view on life , the world ,
everything . you . wow . you've had such an
impact on my lfe and i am thankful and blessed .
and i love you for that . and i love you for many
many things . i love you for you . i love you for
falling in love with me . i love you because it's you
i've fallen in love with . I LOVE YOU ,

d i s t a n c e

puffy eyes , lips and cheeks . dried tears and
stuffy nose . 2 am . still in love with the girl
moving halfway across the country .
distance kills me .
i can barely handle my dad not here , how can i
handle her not here ?
what am i gonna do when she goes ?
i can't just forget about her !
you're gonna remember me , i hope you do .
look at what you've done to me . you made me
fall for you and you're leaving .
i hate but love that i've fallen for you, because
you're amazing and wow . i can just go on about
you .
but i hate it because i'm on limited time with you
..
i want a ' forever '
but what is that ?
i'm hoping that it's you ,
because i want you ,
here ..
with me . holding me . in your arms .
Make our kiss feel never ending .
i promised myself i would try

you said you think we can

i said i want to
we'll make this work .
i want to make this work .
i'm promising myself that i will try . i will try with
all i have in me .
because you i have fallen in love with .
please , one thing i ask ..
don't forget about me .
i don't want to be forgotten
i don't want to be just :
that chick you dated your senior year
No
i want to be :
that chick you're still with since senior year
Yes
that's me .
that's us .
" i wanna slow dance with you in the kitchen late
at night " - elaina
that's going to be us .
you and me .
for as long as possible .

naked for you

hey , do you dare me ?
i'm about to show you all of me
can you handle it ?
don't be scared
tell me you want all of me please

'cause i'm right here
giving every bit of me that i can
can i get all of you ?
half of you isn't enough . i want more .
you're getting the most

following me

you're still there
all the time
even though you say you don't care
and you even claimed you'd be here for a lifetime

but I hate this
please get out of my head
I don't want to be reminded of your kiss
this was the reason i fled

cause you said you needed me
more than i needed you
but i needed you more, maybe
so screw you

why are you in my dreams?
in my photos?
words flowing in a stream
of just pure exposure

get away, get away, get away
stop following me

dream about you

i had a dream about you
you were smiling and laughing
filled with joy and no care in the world
you thanked me
for being good to you
i reminded you that i would always love you
and i still dream about you

i dream about you
doing the most to get attention
about us getting lost in the truck
or kissing while we undressed each other
dreams where i still loved you
and you loved me morer
all in the dream about you

curl up

i want to curl up and forget about you
i want to get rid of every thought about you
i want to forget the memories i had with you
i want to delete without hesitation all the videos of you
i want to burn your things because they still smell like you
i want to curl up and forget about you

curl up
curl up
curl up

forget you
forget you
forget you

delete you
delete you
delete you

curl up
curl up
curl up

i want to curl up and forget the world with you

i want to share every thought with you

i want to make more memories with you

i want to save the embarrassing videos of you

i want to take more pictures with you

i want to curl up and forget the world with you

over you

i'm finally over you
finally over your smile
finally over your scent
finally over your touch
i'm finally over you

your smile doesn't make me smile anymore
your scent makes me want to spray the room with my perfume
your touch is gone, and i don't miss it anymore

i'm finally over you
finally over your laugh
finally over your hands
finally over your presence
i'm finally over you

your laugh doesn't make me laugh anymore
your hands don't beg to be held by mine anymore
your presence bothers me

i'm finally over you
finally over all the dates, we had
finally over all the first, you gave me
finally over the way, you loved me

finally over the love, i gave you
i'm finally over you

i don't miss the dates
i've made new first
i don't miss your love
i don't love you anymore
i'm finally over you

sometimes i

sometimes I, just want to delete you from my life

that way you're not in the way of my
current relationship and happiness

sometimes i think back and say you weren't worth all that time

It sucks that i spent so long on you and
wasted days and months of my life .

but although my life did turn around for the better
, i hate knowing and remembering you .

It's easy to ignore , but how can someone
just forget memories ?

Im okay with the memories there , i just
want all the damn reminders gone .

I want to delete all the reminders of
how you used tp be in my life .

cool , you were here . but i hate that you
left traces of yourself here .

sometimes i just want to delete you from my life .

fucking her.

im glad im happier now .

why

why do i still care about you ? you've moved on
and you're happier now . you're happier now
without me and that's what's honestly killing me .
it's hurting and i hate that you still have
this hold on me that everything you do and say hurts .
you love her and not me and i hate that . i miss
you . i wish we were at least friends . but you
hate me .. and that kills me just as much too .
please leave my mind . leave it . please leave my
heart . please leave . i beg of you to leave .
please , please , please .. go .

go away. let go. say good bye.

don't come back

don't try hanging on

don't say hi anymore

i left

i let go

i said bye

stop coming back

stop hanging on

stop saying hi

im not going back

im not gonna hang on

im not gonna say hi

go away.

let go.

say goodbye.

wish

i wish i was enough for someone

i wish the things i did for people mattered to them .

i wish my love was stronger

i wish i loved harder

i wish the way i cared was better

i wish i had smiled a little bigger

i wish i laughed a bit louder

i wish i held you longer

i wish i learned how to skate , or how to rap or how to cook

i wish i knew how to love , trust , or be jealous .

i wished i mattered to you

i wished i was enough not just for someone

i wished i was enough for you

thank you for being the best ive ever had.

thank you for being the best ive ever had thank you for being my first real love. you showed me what a real and true relationship is, and ill forever be thankful and grateful. thank you for being there to wipe my tears when it was hard to myself. thank you for caring when i didnt. thank you for loving me, when it was hard for you. thank you for being the best i will ever have. even when i left, you loved harder until i made it impossible to ever love me again. thank you for moving on when i couldnt. thank you for finding someone that loves you, when my love wasn't enough anymore.

you're someone i will never forget. the videos are deleted, the pictures are thrown, the notes got burned, but the memories are here. on the smell of your hoodie, with the cologne on my dresser, on your favorite shirt i wore, with the same makeup look you loved on me, on my sheets, in your clothes i wear every other day, on the jewelry i wore with you, the playlist we had together, songs i cant hear again without hearing you sing, at the places we went, in the parking lots we parked for hours. i could never forget. the tears you caught, the hands that held mine, the eyes that glared at me in awe, the smile you gave, the sleepy voice over facetime, the laugh, oh the laugh you have being my favorite sound, your voice singing me to sleep at 2 a.m., calming me down from a panic attack over facetime, giving me a kiss before you left, and another just because.

thank you, for being you. and never changing.

keep getting better. better for her.

and to her, be patient. love her with your all, and wipe her tears and kiss her scars, and hold her till the end

of time. she's better. for you. don't let her go. she's
a diamond. she's the most beautiful sunflower in a
garden of roses. pick her. choose her. love her.

cause i know ill never stop.

her finding of herself

unfold

peel the petals off one by one

don't hurt the flower , it's delicate

but don't prick yourself on the thorns, that's it's only protection

don't get lost in just the beauty of the petals.

be gentle

there's writing inside of the petals

 spilling out it's secrets

don't take advantage

it's a rare flower to find

the core of it is beautiful and unique

no one has seen it for they fear it could be poisonous

be gentle

don't be scared

don't hurt the flower

but don't prick yourself on the thorns, that's it's only protection

is the complexity and rarity driving you in?

come in

i might just unfold myself to you

i might pull the petals back and let them fall in your hands

don't hurt me, i'm delicate

but don't push me, my thorns are my protection

get lost in my beauty

be gentle

i'll unfold

I am not all fear

you've seen my walls
seen my locked doors and covered windows
you've seen the garbage still on the curb
seen the graffiti on my door

but don't let that stop you from walking up the
driveway filled with weeds in the cracks
don't let it stop you from knocking on the
door with no welcome mat below it

my walls come down sometimes
my doors can open, the windows can shine light sometimes too
the garbage won't be on the curb
and the graffiti will be wiped clean sometimes

but it takes a brave person to walk up the
driveway and plant some flowers
it takes a risk taking person to knock on the
door and bring a welcoming heart with them

I am not all fear, it just takes some time to open up
be patient.
I am not all fear.

idc

you wish you were me so bad
just stop honestly
you're stupid
childish and clueless
oblivious to the truth

colors again

i see colors in everyone
everyone i know has a color attached to them
some are two colors, some are just one color
sometimes they even change over time
there's different shades,
there's different tones,
there's colors in everyone
i see colors in everyone

colors again
colors again
colors again

i see colors in everyone
dad's color has always been white, with light brown in it
isaiah's color is a fiery red, with a splash of blue
lynzey's color has changed over so much time,
from red to baby pink and harsh black
my color is orange, a bright orange with hints of white in it
there's different shades
there's different tones
there's colors in everyone
i see colors in everyone

colors again

colors again
colors again

her guardian angel

for leah,
for leaving too soon, but in
heaven she stays

clouds

you're not here
and today that's okay
i think about you everyday
and say a prayer

you're in the clouds
looking down on me, hopefully
you're with the angels
running and singing freely

today isn't a cursed day
it's a blessed day
a day heaven was blessed with a new angel

#runforleah 12.5.14
  12.5.19 | 2:43 p.m.

her hope
for the ones with hope
and my dad, who never lost hope in me,
and my grandma, for giving me hope